# My Struggle,
# My Prayer.

Connecting to God's Word
in the midst of an uncertain time

Tiffany Palmer

# DEDICATION

Thank you to my Lord and Savior, Jesus Christ, for getting me through every struggle. Thank You for keeping Your promise to be present in my life. You are a faithful God.

# ACKNOWLEDGMENTS

Thank you to my husband, Chris, and our four children, Courtney, Peyton, Christian and Evan. Your support through this time has been amazing. You have been the encouragement I needed to keep pressing on each and every day. I can never say thank you enough.
I love you much. You're my favorite family.


There are so many others to thank. God has placed some truly wonderful people in my life. I have both family and friends that are dear to me. Thank you all for believing in me, encouraging me and standing by me. It has meant so very much.

Dear Reader,

This devotional book is written in a format that takes you through a personal journey I am currently facing. It is definietly an uncertain time for me and my family. However, we have seen God's faithfulness over and over throught these last five years.

Each day's devotion describes a specific incident I have faced on this jouney. I then tie that incident in with scripture and close with a prayer. It's a very simply written book, but hopefully will give you insight into how relatable God's word really can be.

What a priviledge it is to share my personal story with you. My hope in writing this book is to encourage you to find hope in any situation through the power of God's word. I am learning more and more of this divine power that is at our disposal, if we just allow God to speak to us and allow the Holy Spirit to operate in and through us.

Sincerely,
Tiffany Palmer

# Day 1

Summer was over, and a new school year had begun! I was an assistant Pre-k teacher and looking forward to another great year with my lead teacher. I know some people are terrified of a Pre-k classroom, but let me tell you, those little ones are so loving, caring, silly and just sponges waiting to absorb all that you have for them. Sure some of them cry as they are being dropped off by mama and daddy into this overwhelming new beginning. But to see them not wanting to leave you by the end of the year makes those first few days so worth it!

So, here we were on day two. The first day had gone about as smoothly as the first day can go. The lead teacher and I were ready for another successful day. But about mid morning, something went wrong. All of the sudden, I couldn't see! I knew the children were next to me. I could feel their presence, pat their heads, hear their voices, but I had no clear vision of them. As they worked away at their centers, I told my lead teacher what was happening. My peripheral vision had gone and my central vision was fading in and out. We called for my husband to come pick me up from the school. We really weren't sure what to do, so we decided to go to the optometrist. They began to ask me if I was experiencing any headaches, nausea or dizziness. But none of those things were present. I felt perfectly fine. After several tests the doctor found that my optic nerve was swollen and suggested an MRI to see if anything else was going on. Finally, about two hours later, my vision returned to me. So strange! What caused this? Will it just randomly happen again? Why wasn't there some kind of warning? So many questions, so few answers.

God has equipped our bodies with the five senses. We use these senses in our everyday life. In fact, we really don't realize we are using them. It's just part of who we are. However, when it comes to our relationship with God, He doesn't necessarily want us to use those senses. He requests that we come to Him by faith. 2 Corinthians 5:7 says "We walk by faith not by sight." God desires for us to put our complete trust in Him even when we can't see what's going on. After I lost my sight at work, I waited on my husband to pick me up and drive me to the doctor. I trusted his hand for security and believed his voice would lead me where I needed to go. I had no doubt he was taking me the right way and that I would be given the care I needed. I never questioned my husband even though I could not clearly see him.

It is the same way with God. He is here for you. There may be a circumstance you are facing that is blinding, almost debilitating. Yet those are the times when we should lean on God's promises all the more.I encourage you to walk by faith, focusing on God and not the circumstance. God is near you and desires to take you where you need to be. Trust in His love for you and believe He has your steps ordered. Listen to His voice as He speaks to you during the storm. Walk with Him even when it's hard to see.

Dear Lord,
Thank You for the incredible body You created. I am in awe of the magnificent detail of each part of the human body. Thank You for the ability to hear laughter, to see the rainbow of colors, to taste the sweetness of flavors, to touch the textures of my surroundings, and to smell the fresh aromas of each new day. These gifts are proof that You are Creator and that You have designed and formed our inner beings. Lord as I walk through this struggle, keep my eyes on You. Increase my faith and trust in You. Teach me to listen for Your voice and to look for Your plan. Draw me closer to You that I may taste of Your goodness. Give me opportunities to touch other people's lives, to share of Your faithfulness. Refresh me with Your sweet presence that I may face this journey with every sense of my being in tune with Yours. I trust You and I choose to walk by faith closely beside You today. Amen.

# Day 2

It was the day after my vision loss episode. I was feeling perfectly fine and since the MRI had not been set up, I decided to go about my normal activities. We made plans to celebrate our youngest son's birthday at a pizza place with family and friends. Though I was still concerned from the previous day's surprise, I put a smile on my face and immersed myself in the  conversation and of course, the pizza. Everything seemed to be going fine and then once again out of nowhere, I started having some trouble again. Only this time it wasn't my vision. Around nine o'clock, the left side of my face began to tighten. At first it wasn't painful. It was almost like I could just feel the muscles kinda twitching, tightening and releasing. Then the pain started to increase and I starting to panic. Not wanting anyone to know, I calmly told my husband Chris that it was time to go. Once we arrived home, I went straight to bed. The unknown of what was happening had me locked up in fear. I didn't want to worry anybody, so I just went to sleep praying all would be well in the morning.

So often in our lives we hide our pain, our hurts, our fears. We think that it will all just go away as if it will evaporate like a drop of water on a hot summer's day. But, that's not how God intended for us to handle our problems. Oh, I'm guilty of it just like you, and I don't know why. Because the greatest freedom, peace and joy I have ever felt in my life is when I have
fully released the junk hoarded inside me to the great care taker of my soul. Psalm 38 is a cry from David over the heavy burden of sin he is carrying. In verse nine, David said "Lord all my desire is before you and my sighing is not hidden from you." As much as we would like to pretend we are fine, God sees the struggle on the inside. It is not hidden from Him. Maybe nobody else can see it, but He can. David cried out to God because he knew this. He knew God could see his pain, cared about his pain and could comfort him during the pain. So, he cried out. When we cry out to God it moves him closer to our situation. It prompts the character of Father that is in Him to hold His child a little tighter. It prompts the comforter in the Holy Spirit to speak the words we need to hear reminding us of His ever presence. It prompts Jesus to stand on our behalf and cry out with us to our God.

Psalm 55:22 says, "Cast your burden on the Lord and He shall sustain you." In order for God to take action to sustain us, we must first take action by casting the burden. We do not serve a passive God. No! We serve a God who desires to take action to defeat anything that comes against us no matter what it may be. Sin, fear, doubt, feelings of rejection and defeat. It doesn't matter. God desires for us to know victory over all circumstances. And though the night may last a little longer than we would like, never underestimate God's ability to step in at any time and speak peace to the storm. He is ready to act, to sustain us. Are we ready and willing to let him? Never keep bundled up what God has the ability to take away. He loves you and desires to heal you from the inside out.

Dear Lord,
We are told in Your word that You have formed us and created us and that You know our inner being. In Your great wisdom, You are able to see and know our thoughts and our fears. You are able to see the depth of our hearts. I ask You, Holy Spirit, to prompt me to come before the throne ready and willing to cast all my burdens before You. To stop playing hide and seek with God and trust His strength to sustain me. Give me the ability to take action against my hidden fears before they take action against me. Come to me, oh God, right here where I am and call my name just as You called out to Adam and Eve in the garden. Clothe me in Your righteousness. May the only hiding place I have be in the shelter of Your outstretched arms. Thank You for being strong enough to carry my burdens, loving enough to wipe my fears away and Father enough to make things new. I love You and seek you today. Amen.

Saturday morning did not start out as I had hoped. My face was still tight, but when I looked in the mirror it was not at all noticeable. However, something else was very noticeable and extremely shocking. My left hand was curled up and no matter how hard I tried, I could not get it to relax. So many emotions rushed over me. I didn't feel bad at all. What in the world could be happening to me?? But again, I hid everything from Chris.(Apparently, I didn't read yesterday's devotion.) After all, we had a meeting that morning and a much needed, long overdue, grocery trip to make.(We have four kids!) No time for this nonsense my body was giving me. I looked in the mirror, gave myself a pep talk and said, "let's do this." Determined to face the day and defeat this crisis on my own, I flung open the bathroom door and marched out like a boss. Unfortunately, I wouldn't be able to hide it or handle it for very long. At the meeting, Chris noticed I was on edge and a couple of times even asked if I was okay. When we finally got home, I knew I had to tell him. He was silent. Scared maybe, but definitely silent. After a long stare he asked if we needed to go to the hospital to which I quickly responded an emphatic NO. The MRI for my vision loss episode was set for Monday, so I figured we could just wait until then. But, he was quick to tell me if I got worse we were going no questions asked. He told me to stay in bed, get some rest and not worry about the kids. He said he would take care of everything.

What a picture of Jesus. Can't you hear Him gently saying, "You rest while I take care of everything"? Yes, I know there are times we need to be actively working for the kingdom and providing for the needs of our family and for others. But, there are also times for rest. Not laziness. Rest. There is a difference. Jesus tried to explain this to Martha in Luke 10:38-42. Martha was distracted by much while Mary was at rest. Mary was doing what we were all created to do. She was taking advantage of the time when she could simply sit at the feet of Jesus and rest. In fact, Jesus even says in verse 42 that this is the one thing that is needed and that Mary had chosen it. Did you catch that?? It is needed. Time with Jesus without distraction is needed. Not demanded of us as Christ followers, not put on a resume in heaven for us to rack up points. No. It's just simply needed.

I could have told Chris, no I can't rest. I need to wash clothes, clean the bathrooms, pull the weeds, etc. (and that would have been true.) But that wasn't what I needed to do at that moment. The sooner we learn that God has the universe spinning in perfect order and that it will not stop even if we do, then we will be able to rest at the feet of Jesus and hear His sweet voice speaking to us. I encourage you today to say yes to time spent with Jesus. Well, really I encourage myself to do so as well. I am as guilty as the next person about not getting in the word as often as I should. I let life get in the way. To be more specific, I let TV get in the way. I let sports get in the way. I let family and friends get in the way. I let sleep get in the way. Do I need to keep going??? Good. Cause I'm feeling pretty rotten right about now. But that's not my goal. God doesn't want you or I to feel bad about ourselves. Nope. But He does want us to know He loves us and desires a special fellowship that can only be found when everything else is put aside. We need that time. Time spent thanking Him for all He has done. Time spent praising Him for his goodness. Time spent listening to His voice for His direction. And time to lift my needs and the needs of others before a God who truly cares. Yes. It is needed. Why? Because in those precious moments we find strength to face the day, comfort for the heartache, hope for a brighter tomorrow and we experience a love like we have never known.

Dear Jesus,
Thank You so much for saying it's okay to rest at Your feet. I have become so busy that I often feel guilty for taking time to stop my daily activities to spend time with You. Forgive me for thinking that time spent with You is a waste or that it should be done quickly so I can move on with my day. Nothing in this world should come before You because nothing in this world is more valuable. When my heart is at its resting rate, that means it is functioning normally. Though it's at rest, the heart is still completing the task it was created to do. Help me to realize that only when I am at rest in You can I function properly and carry out the tasks You have given me to do. Help me to remember that often times when I have no idea what is happening the best thing to do is rest in the One who does. Only when I rest in You can I find the strength and hope to face each day. Amen.

Day 4

Saturday and Sunday all I did was rest. Even during sunday school (small group they call it now) I was quiet, which if you knew me, you would know that's not normal. So when the alarm sounded Monday morning and the symptoms were still present, we knew something had to be done. We sent the kids to school, and then I went to school to explain to my administrator and lead teacher what had been going on over the weekend. Then Chris and I headed straight to my doctor. From that moment on, Monday became a whirlwind. A whirlwind that landed me in the hospital, a place I did not want to be.

In the middle of all this commotion, another change starting happening in my body. My legs became very weak and my left arm began to jerk violently and uncontrollably. And though my hand was no longer curled up, it was tight and stiff with each finger in a curled, yet cramped, position. The entire left side of my body seemed to be operating on its own. And while I was trying to comprehend what was happening, I was being wheeled from one testing room to another. The peaceful state of rest I was in over the weekend had quickly turned into a storm.

In Mark 4:35-41, we read of a raging storm the disciples were facing while out at sea. Just hours before, they were resting on land, listening to the teachings of Jesus. But in a moment, things changed. The storm was so strong that the winds were beating them down and the waves were crashing in and filling the boat. The disciples began to cry out to Jesus. The storm they were facing caused great chaos on the inside of them. So great, that they felt compelled to cry out to Jesus. "JESUS" they frantically called. But where was He? Weren't we just with Him? Isn't He in the boat?? "JESUS!!!! Can You hear us??" And suddenly there He was. Coming up from the bottom of the boat. He had been sleeping through the storm. Probably stretching and yawning while coming up the stairs, He reached the edge of the boat, raised His arms and spoke peace to the storm. The winds and the waves immediately obeyed and all was calm again.

One thing I love about the Bible is that it is relevant to my life. I mean I have never been out on the sea and faced a fierce storm such as the disciples did. But I sure have faced some raging storms in my life that I didn't think I would survive. Storms that made me cry out to Jesus. Storms that hit just like the one I was in now. Storms that just come out of nowhere and BAM!!
We do not know what life has in store for us. Some people seem to have smooth sailing their whole life. Others can't seem to get a break from the

14

crashing waves. And then I would say there are some like me. Those who seem to have blue skies and then suddenly the eye of the hurricane is swirling around close in sight. No matter which category you may find yourself in, just know that Jesus loves you. He doesn't love one group more than the other. You aren't super spiritual just because all your skies are sunny. You're not a failure as a follower if the storms are raging. I mean, look, the disciples had just been feeding on the word of God. They had been in fellowship with Him. They were such good friends with Him that He was in the boat with them! All I know is that it is to our advantage to have the calmer of the sea along with us on this journey of life. Maybe we don't know what's coming, but He does. And all He has to do is raise His hands and speak peace to the storm. That's who I want in my boat!


Dear Jesus,

What a comfort to know that You are sovereign over life's raging storms. I am so thankful I serve a God who holds tomorrow and all that it brings. Nothing surprises You and nothing surpasses You! Lord I give you power over this ship, over this earthly vessel of mine. Be the captain of my life and help me to sail on the waters with You. Help me to trust in You even when I see the storm clouds gather, for You are over them all. Thank you for the stories in the scripture that show me, You were God back then and You are still God today. In You and You alone there is peace in the storm. In Jesus' name, Amen.

# Day 5

Chris and I had been at the hospital all day long! Finally I was told I was being admitted. Chris decided to go home, get the kids settled and gather some of my belongings. Being admitted to the hospital was not on my list of things to do that day. Suddenly I was overwhelmed with frustration. I was in a place I had no desire to be. I mean, I realize nobody likes being in the hospital, but I REALLY don't like being there! Just the thought of an IV sends chills up my spine!
But honestly, admitted to the hospital was what I needed. Did I just say that??? Yes. Yes, I did. You see the truth is I had no idea what was happening to my body, so the hospital was exactly where I needed to be. We had no idea what the outcome would be. We had no idea if I would ever be the same. We were lost. So I needed to be in the hands of someone who could save me.

It's times like this when I stop and ask myself if I am truly in the hands of the One who can save. There is only one set of hands that can truly save anybody. Those are the nail-pierced hands of Jesus. All it takes is for us to admit ourselves into His care. In John chapter 14:6, Jesus tells us that He is the way, the truth and the life. He is the way to salvation, the true healer and restorer of our souls and the very life we breathe now and for eternity.

Sometimes here on earth we find ourselves in places or situations we don't want to be in. I don't want to endure that kind of miserable feeling for an eternity. So, for me, Hell is not an option. I have no desire to be there. And I don't want you to be there either. So, if you have not admitted yourself into the loving, caring, very capable hands of Jesus, I beg you to do so right now! Only Jesus can save you from the pit of hell and restore a right relationship with you and God the Father. His shed blood was freely poured out to cover your sins. He can and will begin a new work in your life. And for those that are saved, maybe you're in a place that is uncomfortable and trying right now. I encourage you to remember the joy of your salvation and ask the Holy Spirit to minister to you during this time. He is faithful to meet all of our needs. And the greatest of those needs is salvation.

Dear Father,

I thank You for the many men and women You have called to be physicians and nurses. I thank You for the hospitals and technology available to help make us well. But ultimately all of us have one illness that needs to be healed and can only be healed by You. That illness is sin. And no doctor, nurse, hospital machine or anything here on earth can save us from that illness. Only Jesus can. Thank You Father for sending Your one and only son to save us. Thank You Jesus for being willing to sacrifice Your life on the cross so that we could be saved. You have rescued us from enduring the penalty of our sin. You have given us eternal life and a renewed relationship with the Father. Because of Your resurrection, we can rise above the pain and sufferings of this life and have a hope in the great things You have planned for us. I ask today that You exercise Your salvation power and save the one who has cried out to You, as well as resurrect the joy of our salvation, that we may celebrate life in You. Amen.

## Day 6

So there I was, alone. Alone in the emergency room. All alone. When Chris left, I felt so isolated. My mama, daddy, siblings and grandparents all live over an hour away. And even though I have precious friends, I didn't want to take them away from their children on a school night. All I could think was I'm all alone and I have no idea what is happening to me. The thoughts of not being able to have someone by my side during this time of uncertainty became so overwhelming, I began to just cry. I guess I was crying out of fear, frustration and did I mention, loneliness.

But then the door began to slowly open. My sadness quickly turned to great hopefulness! Who was it going to be?? Did somebody from my family really come all this way so late and on such short notice? Or maybe it was a close friend who had dropped everything to come and check on me. I was so hoping for a familiar face, like maybe my mama. (You're never too old for your mom!) And then I saw the face peeking in as if to make sure it was okay to come in. No, it wasn't a family member or even a close friend. It was a total stranger. A janitor was coming in the room to take out the trash. For a moment, I felt so let down and the tears started flowing again. But you know, that Janitor, he noticed my tears. And once we locked eyes, I could see compassion in him. Not sure why, but I apologized for my tears and quickly wiped them away. His response? "Don't apologize. It's going to be ok. God is with you." I will never forget his words. Words he didn't have to say, but because he did, a calmness came over me. The timing and the message was absolutely amazing! His words were exactly what I needed to hear! God saw my need. He heard my cry. He sent a messenger to remind me that He will never leave me nor forsake me. I wasn't alone in that hospital. No. God was right there with me. I'm so thankful for that janitor!! I'm so thankful for his willingness to be used by God. It made a huge impact on me.

In the New Testament, Paul was always spreading the gospel. Even during times of imprisonment, he took time to write letters to the churches. His main goal? He wanted to encourage his fellow brothers and sisters in Christ. In Second Thessalonians 1, we see Paul thanking God for his fellow christians, encouraging them to press on despite the trials. He prayed blessings over them for their journeys. Like Paul, we are given opportunities to speak blessings and encouragement into the lives of other people. I'm not sure what Paul was going through at the time he wrote this, but chances are he was in the midst of a struggle as well. Yet he took the time to make a difference in the life of someone else. We are called to do the same. As we go about our daily routines,

God will often put people in our paths to reach out to, just as the janitor did for me. Is there someone you could encourage today? If so, be willing to go and trust God to give you the words. It can even be something as simple as "It's going to be ok. God is with you".

Dear Father,
Thank You for looking at us with compassion and touching our hearts with Your tender voice. Thank You for the examples we have in scripture of others living out that same compassion in their lives. Sometimes we get so caught up in ourselves, we don't think of others as we should. Acts 10:38 says that Jesus went about doing good. I pray as we go about our daily routines sometimes even surrounded by garbage in our own life, that You, Holy Spirit will open our eyes to see the needs of those around us. Help us to stop our business and be about Your business. To speak words of life and hope to the hurting and words of promise to the ones in despair. Equip us with compassion, love and mercy so that we may diligently serve the precious lives of those You have placed in our paths. Amen.

Day 7

Finally around midnight, I was moved out of the ER and into a regular room. My first thought was just try to go to sleep and maybe when I wake up this nightmare will be over. Let me be real honest here. That never happened. Because, I had finally been put on a floor, the nurses had to check my vital signs and ask me all kinds of questions about my health history. And I do mean ALL!!! Are you serious?? Does it really have to be done at midnight?? (Of course I wasn't verbalizing this. Just thinking it very loudly in my head!!)

Now if the nurses had been more like Jesus, they would have just known all about me and nobody's precious time or hours of sleep would have been taken. I know you're laughing, but I'm serious! Look at John 4:5-42. I know that's a lot, but just read it. Like right now. I'll wait for you to finish.

Finished?? OK. Isn't it amazing that Jesus knew *all* about the woman at the well? I mean, if there were health history questions, he could have answered those too! Jesus carried on this long conversation with this woman revealing everything in her life. What had happened and what was happening now. Wow! But, Jesus doesn't do this to be arrogant. No, that isn't Jesus' character. He did this to reveal Himself to this woman. He wanted her to know He is all knowing. He wanted her to know, He is God.

After this life changing experience with Jesus, the woman hurries away to share with the city folks that Jesus told her *all* she ever did. I'm sure some of the people knew *some* of her life history. But *all*? For me personally I would love to leave the "all" out of that statement. And maybe that woman did too. You see, my health history may be okay, but my spiritual history could use some surgery! I wouldn't want everyone to know the "all." Get what I'm saying? And, I'm sure this woman must have felt this way at first. But after receiving this life changing water, this woman, like me, was so glad Jesus knew her history. ALL her history. But even more importantly, she was glad He knew her future. He knew what she could become if she would only partake of this life giving water. You see He is the only one who can perform successful heart surgery. He can take what we were and make us into something new. No questions asked. Jesus knows us better than we know ourselves. So like this woman, it is wise for us to trust Him with our lives (past, present and future.)

Dear Jesus,

With the demands of being a spouse, a parent, an employee, a friend and some days it seems so much more, I get tired of all the questions. I get tired of being the one to try and solve a problem or give the answer someone wants to hear. So, Lord Jesus, I thank You for those times I can come before You and rest in the One who knows it all. I am thankful that when I come to You there isn't a long list of questions for me to answer, there is just revelation. I pray Psalm 139:23-24. "Search me, O God, and know my heart. Try me and know my anxieties; and see if there be any wicked way in me. And lead me in the way everlasting." Lord, I come to You like the woman at the well, with a past, but with a hope. I believe You will reveal Yourself to me, break my chains and give me a testimony to share. And I believe that because You are changing me, others will see Your glory instead of my history and come to that living water, never to thirst again. Thank you God. In Jesus' name. Amen.

# Day 8

The next day, my first full day in the hospital, began the worse part of my experience. I have never liked having blood drawn, so when the time came, let's just say I was not a happy camper. By now, my jerking movements were more frequent, very strong and extremely violent. I was randomly hitting the bed railing, kicking the footboard and even gave myself the one-two punch. Anything that was near me was in the line of fire! No longer was it limited to my left side. By now, my entire body was out of control. So when the nurse came to draw blood, you would have thought I was under some sort of attack! Already fearful of needles and now these freaky movements. I was a basket case to say the least. I'm sure it was quite the scene to behold. Who knew that drawing blood could cause so much drama?

Jesus. Jesus knew. Jesus knew that spilled blood would cause the greatest scene of drama known to this world. He knew the agony of the cross would cause a movement more intense than any movement I was experiencing. And He chose to play the leading role. Why? Because, He loves His Father and He loves you and me. Jesus wanted to reunite Father and child, so He chose to sacrifice His life in order to make that happen. Hebrews 9:22-28 explains that without the shedding of blood there is no remission for sin. In order to find out what was wrong with me, they had to draw my blood. That is where my remission would begin. So, it is with our disease of sin. The only way to heal us is by the drawing of blood. Jesus was willing to make that sacrifice so that we would be free from sin and joined again with the Father. He was the only one pure enough and holy enough to accomplish this remission. Only the blood of Jesus.

Dear Jesus,

Today I thank You for Your precious shed blood. I thank You for enduring the agony of the cross. I thank You for living a holy and blameless life so that Your sacrifice could be my cure. I choose to believe Your blood was spilled on my behalf. I choose to believe that Your blood has the power to save, to cleanse, to wash away any and all disease. Because of You, Jesus, I can be reunited with my Creator, my Father. I pray for those that have not accepted Your sacrifice. I pray today they would realize You are the way, the truth, the life. That Your blood still has cleansing power today. That there is salvation, hope, healing and remission through You, Jesus. Only through You. Amen.

Day 9

By the afternoon, my eventful morning of testing and blood being sucked away from me had somewhat settled down. But, little did I know, some of the greatest pain was yet to come. Chris left to go pick up the children from school so they could see me for the first time in almost two days. I was so excited to see them, but was also nervous about how they would react. My condition had changed and worsened so quickly. I was not the same mom that had seen just a day or so ago.As they slowly came in, my heart was broken. I will never forget the looks on their faces, their hesitancy to enter the room or the tears that began streaming down Courtney's face. She is our oldest, our only daughter. She had to quickly step in the restroom to try and regroup before coming to my bedside. But, there was no regrouping. As she neared my bed, the tears flowed continuously. Uncertainty, fear and just sheer brokenness caused her to weep for her mama.

The shortest verse in the Bible is John 11:35. It simple says, "Jesus wept." Lazarus was the brother of Mary and Martha. All three of them were dearly loved by Jesus. Their friendship was very special. So when Lazarus became sick the ladies knew Jesus would want to know. They quickly sent word to Him. But, by the time He got into town, Lazarus had passed away. Upon arriving and seeing the tomb, Jesus wept.

When entering my room, Courtney saw that some sort of illness had invaded my body and was causing much pain and weariness. And, she wept. She knew that this wasn't how I was suppose to be. She knew I was being gripped by something terrible. So, she wept. Arriving at the graveside, Jesus saw the same thing. He saw the grip that sin has on us. Romans 6:23 says the wages of sin is death. Physical and spiritual death entered our world the moment sin entered. Jesus knew this, and He was heartbroken. He was weeping, not just for Mary, Martha and Lazarus, but for us all. For me. For you. He wasn't weeping because there was no hope for Lazarus. He knew He was the hope of glory. But God's heart breaks for us when He sees the sin that entangles us and leads to death, to separation from Him. So, to give hope to everyone around, to establish right then and there the power He has over sin and death, Jesus called Lazarus out of that tomb. He does the same thing today. Jesus is calling us to come away from the things of this world that hold us down, that bind us up and ultimately lead to death. He is calling us to live a resurrected life filled with compassion for Him and for others.

Dear Jesus,
You are a Savior who has pity on us. Yet, You desire for us to be raised above the pitiful state of sin and be resurrected into new life with You. Thank You for having enough compassion and love for us that we are not left alone to die. Give me the strength to walk away from the grip of sin. To say "No" to the things of this world and "Yes" to You. I pray each day I will use eyes of compassion to see the needs of others. May I be willing to share the gospel with those around me so they too can be loosed from the death of sin. Thank You for Your love and for Your power over sin and death. Thank You for calling me out of death and into life. You are my Savior! Amen.

It was more difficult seeing my children than I realized it would be. I really thought it would have been joyous, but the fear in their eyes broke my heart. While Courtney dried her tears, Peyton, Christian and Evan just stared at me. Not really any words to be said, not any moves to be made. They were frozen in the moment. With blank faces and fake smiles, they were afraid to touch or even look at their mom in this disturbing condition. As the clocked ticked by, eventually they became less like ice sculptures and more like my children. But, it took every smile and empty conversation I could come up with to melt their frozen bodies. As their mother, I felt it was my job to make them feel like everything was okay.

I imagine Adam and Eve had the same blank look on their faces as they left the garden of Eden. A look of disbelief in what was happening. Their place of peace, harmony and refuge suddenly snatched away from them because of a disease - sin. They knew the choice to disobey would lead to death, but they gambled anyway. God placed judgement on them that very day and lead them out of the garden. But, before leading them out, God, being the Father that He is, wanted to assure them that everything would be right again some day. He did what seemed to be a very simple act, but one that shows His love and care for us as His children. Genesis 3:21 tells us that God clothed Adam and Eve. God did it to show them that though you have sinned against Me, I still love you. I still desire to be your Refuge, your Provider, your Father. I imagine each day as they looked at their attire, they were reminded of that. God can take a most basic thing such as clothing and tell a story of redemption.

That day in the hospital, I tried, as any parent would do, to make a seemingly unbearable situation much easier to bear. God does the same and more for His children. He sees our despair, and being the good Father that He is, has reached out to us with mercy. His word gives us hope and healing so that our looks of disbelief can become expressions of pure joy.

Dear Father,
Thank You for looking upon me as Your child, Your beloved one. Help me to understand Your love for me. And may this understanding cause a great desire to rise up within me to honor You with my life. I know that because of the sacrifice of Jesus, I can be clothed in Your righteousness. Thank you for taking the basic things in life and using them to remind me of the great love and mercy You have for me. You are indeed the greatest Father anyone could ever have. I praise You and thank You for that. Amen.

# Day 11

Nighttime in a hospital can be lonely and almost depressing. So, I decided to focus on the upcoming morning and the gentle touches it would bring. You see each night Chris went home to be with the children to keep things as normal as possible. Then, in the mornings, he would take them to school, go check on things at work and then come to be by my side. Whenever he walked in, a calmness would come over me. I loved looking into his deep brown eyes seeing his handsome face. It let me know everything would be alright. Okay, let me stop there. It's getting too mushy. I know, I know. But, I do have to say this. His touches were the best. Holding his hand brought me security. His strong arms wrapping around me gave me encouragement. And the softness of each stroke gliding down my hair gave me peace. He touched me. Oh, he touched me. And, oh the joy that floods my soul.

I just imagine, though not recorded in Scripture, that in Matthew 8:3, for the first time that song was sung as Jesus reached out and touched the leper. When approaching Jesus the leper only asked to be made clean, not necessarily to be touched. Jesus could have healed him with words only, no touching involved. But, I believe that day, Jesus knew the leper desperately wanted a touch. It probably had been many days, perhaps years, since he felt the warmth of a touch. Jesus, out of His great love for the leper, stretched out his arm and gave him what he desperately needed most; a touch.

Chris never had to touch me. He could have kept his distance and encouraged me from the sidelines. But, each morning he touched me. Those touches gave me hope to face the day. He was the hands of Jesus for me. Jesus has a desire to reach out to you and bless you with the touch of His hands. If you will allow Him, I promise you will never be the same. If Jesus wasn't afraid to touch the leper, He isn't afraid to touch you. No matter what circumstance has stricken you, no matter where you may find yourself, He wants to reach out and give you what you need most. A touch. A touch that can bring healing, forgiveness, peace, and a great joy that will flood your soul.

Dear sweet Jesus,
Oh, how I need your touch! I beg you today to reach out to me. I feel abandoned and beyond hope at times. But, one touch from You can bring me sweet relief. One touch from you can cure any pain, any suffering, any rejection and any sense of worthlessness. Grant me faith to believe in Your touch and to hope in Your healing. May I one day be used by You to touch someone else who desperately needs You. Amen.

# Day 12

I have a confession to make. It's one that I can't keep a secret any longer. Please don't throw away this devotion book when you start to read this. Please, please finish reading. My confession is this. There is another man involved. My husband Chris means so much to me, but because we have four children and he has a job, he just couldn't be with me the whole day. But this man could be. And believe me, he was. It was my father-in-law. Whew! Glad I got that off my chest. No, seriously. My father-in-law would not leave. It was kinda weird and even a little bit awkward. But, no matter what, he wouldn't go anywhere. What makes this so strange is that he is not that type of father-in-law. He is normally by himself. He isn't married and he would rather be out on the road working than hanging around the house or especially a hospital. Nothing wrong with that. It's just his personality. So, to have him in the hospital room almost 24/7 was totally not the norm.

In Ruth 1:16-17, we see this same kind of commitment. It would have made sense for Ruth to go back to her homeland. Every man in the household she had married into was dead, Naomi, her mother-in-law, released her and even encouraged her to go back. But Ruth saw the pain Naomi was carrying and knew she needed someone by her side. Ruth didn't know what the future held for either of them, but she knew together they would be alright. I believe my father-in-law could see that I wanted someone to be with me, without me even saying a word. So, he made the necessary sacrifices to help me in my time of need. Like Ruth, he put himself aside and made a commitment to help me along my journey.

I don't believe we were meant to do life alone. Whether you are married or you're single, young or old, there is someone out there you can partner with and encourage along life's journey. I challenge you today to be a Ruth. To commit to praying for a friend and standing by them no matter what circumstance may come. May we be people who do not quickly flee when trouble comes, but people who stand firm and walk along side the broken, the tired and the weary, letting them know they have a companion, a faithful friend. May we allow Jesus to shine through us giving them a hope to press on. Sometimes, when we don't know what to say, just being there can make all the difference. I know that's what my father-in law did for me. Not many words were exchanged during those hospital days, but he was there. May we have that same commitment for the one God has placed in our life.

Dear Father,

Thank You that I do not have to do life alone. You are faithfully committed to staying by my side no matter the circumstance I am facing. Even when I have neglected to acknowledge You and at times encouraged you to leave, you still stay with me. Thank You for such a deep level of commitment. I ask that you would instill that same level of commitment in me. Give me the desire to stay by Your side, to dig deeper into Your word and to live everyday in the light of Your love. Help me, Father, to be more committed to the people You have placed in my life. To be mindful of their needs and to bless them by showing Your love. Give me the strength to stand along side them through life's journey. Thank you for this day. I pray I use it to glorify you. Amen.

Day 13

Finally, Thursday morning came!! What's so great about Thursday you ask? I got to sign the form. You know the release form. Thank you, Jesus! I get to go home! But honestly, on one hand I was happy to be leaving because I was so ready to get all the wires off me, get the poking over with and that blood pressure cuff was really checking my nerves! But on the other hand, it meant going home in the same condition with no answers. Frustrated? You could say so. I mean I just wanted to find out what was wrong, get the correct medication and go on with my life. I didn't need an infirmity. Or did I?

2 Corinthians 12:7-10 tell us about an infirmity that Paul had. We read that Paul had a "thorn in the flesh". Verse 7 says that this "thorn" was given to him to keep him humble. Yet, he still asked God to remove it. Not once. Not twice. But three times Paul pleaded with God for it to be removed. But after all the asking and all the pleading, Paul still had a thorn in the flesh. Sounds familiar? I mean after all the testing and the blood work and the questions and the long days and nights in the hospital and the prayers, I still have this??

If you stop reading at verse 7 or 8, you might start to feel sorry for Paul. And, if you stopped reading this devotional right now you might feel sorry for me too. But read verse 9. Read it again. God's grace is sufficient. His strength is perfect. And, through the infirmity, the power of Christ may rest upon me. Those are some very powerful words! Please understand me, I don't want to be sick. I don't want to have these freakish jerking movements, these random falls, the slurred speech and on and on. I want my body to function, normally. But to know that no matter what my physical body is going through, that I, like Paul, can have the grace of God, the strength of God and the power of Christ resting upon me. Wow!! That changes everything. No longer do I choose to look at the circumstance, but I choose to look at what God can do through the circumstance.

Life can sure throw some blows. And, there are times we beg God for the storm to subside,for the thorn to be removed. And let's be honest, sometimes it just doesn't happen. But that doesn't mean He isn't God. No. Not at all. I am learning that those are the times God reveals more to me about who He is and what His character is like. I am learning that no matter the mystery ahead of me, I am in the hands of the all knowing. I am in the hands of the one who holds my future. And, because I choose to believe that He is God and He will display His strength through the trial, I like Paul will boast in the seemingly uncomfortable circumstance

32

so that the power of Christ may rest upon me and draw me and others nearer to God.

Dear God,
We are a fast-paced world that wants everything immediately, including answers. God I pray today that You would change my heart concerning this. Teach me Lord to rest in the fact that because You are all-knowing, I don't have to be. Give me the faith to believe Your words, that Your grace truly is sufficient and Your strength is perfect enough to carry me through anything. May the power of Christ rest upon me giving me the courage to face whatever may come my way. Thank you God for Your presence in my life. Amen.

# Day 14

How do I even begin this entry? Even though it's been almost two years since the upcoming described incident occurred, the pain in the memory is still so very real and so very strong. I was home from the hospital. I was sitting on the edge of the bed ready for Chris to cover me up for a good night's rest. Then the phone rang. If you don't know me personally, this part may not mean much to you at all. But if you know me then you will understand.

My Papa called. Normally when he called, I hung up with a big smile on my face. But that would not be the case this time. His words cut my heart so deeply the pain was unbearable. My Papa told me he would not come see me until I got better. He said the family had told him how bad I really was and he couldn't bear to see me like that. His words were "You just got to get better so I can see you." Devastated, I hung up the phone. My body began to shake and the tears were unlike any rain storm ever experienced. Chris had to literally hold me down to get my body still and threatened to take me right back to the hospital if I couldn't calm down and breathe. It sounds harsh but I needed him to do that at that very moment or I would have been completely broken. The thought of not seeing my Papa again and having him smile at me and tell me he loves me, it was just too much pain for me at that time.

Jesus must have felt that same pain but at a much greater magnitude when He cried out on the cross "My God, my God why have You forsaken Me." I may be wrong, but I don't think it says in scripture that God turned away. I know many have said that's what happened, but I couldn't find it. But do I believe that's what happened? Yes! Why do I believe that? Because God so loves. He is a Father who deeply loves His children. And I do believe the pain, the suffering and all that nasty ugly sin that was placed on Jesus was too much for even our great God. Because His child was in pain so was He.

When I think of that it makes my conversation with Papa more clear to me. Papa was broken when I was broken. He wept when I wept. He was hurting when I was hurting. My Papa loved me. And because he loved me he wouldn't be able to keep his head turned for long. We did end up spending much more time together despite my condition. And during those moments he prayed for me, he laughed with me and sometimes at me. He rejoiced with me when I had a good day. He was there with me. Because he loves me he couldn't leave me no matter what condition I was in.

Maybe God did turned his head in that brief moment in time. I don't know for sure. But I know this,He did not keep it turned. He is looking down on us now watching over us with a loving heart that cannot even begin to be measured. Psalm 8:4 says that God is mindful of us and He gives attention to us. God has the entire universe to maintain. He has a host in heaven to oversee. And the construction of new mansions are happening every day. But He is mindful of me. He is mindful of you. He is paying attention to us right now. Oh, how He loves us. No matter our circumstance, no matter our condition, God Almighty is looking at us thinking about us and attending to us.


Dear Father
Thank You for being an active Father. You don't stand on the sidelines too busy to watch over me. No, You're not like that. You are right here with me engaging in every aspect of my life. Your eyes are ever upon me and Your mind is set on me. What a privilege it is to have a Father like You. Your love is unconditional and Your presence is never far away. Please forgive me for the times my sin gets in the way of our relationship. I ask You to forgive me and put me back in right standing with You that we may walk together in peace. Amen.

# Day 15

Over the next few days, I began to experience another frustrating setback. Several times when walking in the house and sometimes when I was just standing, my legs would give out and I would fall. I never really got hurt, but it wasn't a comfortable feeling physically or emotionally. One time, it happened right after lunch. We were getting up from the table after eating, and I knew I felt weak. Chris and Courtney were right by my side. But all of the sudden I hit the floor. Again, didn't get hurt but sat there for a split-second getting ready to have a pity party. Only for a split second though. Why wasn't I there longer? Because I was quickly lifted back up by the two loved ones by my side. Galatians 6:1 talks about helping someone when they have fallen. Now I know it is talking about when they have fallen into sin but let's make the connection. The truth is everyone falls. We can all probably get a chuckle out of a time in our past when we have embarrassingly fallen. However when we fall into sin it is no longer a laughing matter. But we all do it. Remember, "We have all sinned and fallen short of the glory of God," Romans 3:23 says. But when we fall there is restoration through Jesus and we can play a part in that process.

In order for me to be restored to a standing position, I needed Chris and Courtney to lift me back up. I wasn't strong enough to get back on my own. But they were. They had steady legs and strong arms. They were not struggling to stand as I had been, so they were in a position to help me. As members of the body of Christ we need to be mindful of our position. If we are standing firm and steady in the faith, then we are to be lifting others out of sin restoring them to their right position in Christ. If we are the ones who have fallen, then we need to be aware of the brothers and sisters who are reaching out their hands to help pick us back up. So where are you? Have you fallen into sin and desperately need a brother or sister to come along and help you? Or are you walking closely with the Lord and able to help the fallen? Be willing to honestly evaluate your position and either get help or provide some help. Jesus longs to restore the fallen into a right position with Him and what a joy it is to take part in this process.

Dear Lord,
I ask today that You show me my position. If there is any sin in my life, I ask that You reveal it to me, set me free from it, forgive me of it, and restore me to right standing with You. If today I am standing firmly with You, then I thank You for this ability to stand, for it is only by Your grace I'm able to do so. But show me, Lord, a fellow brother or sister that I can love, encourage and lift up so that they too may stand with me before You. Thank you for sending others to walk alongside me in this journey. Help me, Lord, to be a faithful servant to You and to those around me. Amen.

# Day 16

After three weeks of no answers, no relief and no change we decided it was time to go somewhere else to find help. It was obvious something was wrong with my body. I was unable to function normally in any way. I couldn't be a mother, a wife and could not even think of returning to work. Even though it only been three weeks, it felt like much much longer. And once discouragement started setting in, we knew something had to be done. So at this point we were willing to go to whatever lengths to get an answer and to get back to living. We knew that just sitting where we were was not the answer.

Have you ever been there? I mean have you ever been in a situation, a circumstance where you knew you didn't belong? A place you knew you couldn't stay? Sometimes it can take awhile for us to see we need to move on. For Jonah it took three days.

In the Book of Jonah Chapters 1 and 2, we see that Jonah decides to run from the Lord's commandment, and that my friend can never land you in a good spot. Jonah ended up in the belly of a whale. One word, disgusting. Okay maybe a few more. Gross. Sickening, skin crawling, ugly face making, smelly, absolutely no other way around it disgusting! Why did it take Jonah three days to realize, "Hey, not the place I need to be." It wouldn't have taken me three seconds, or would it? Sometimes in our pride, stubbornness or dare I say sinful nature we don't want to move. We think we are fine just as we are. But the truth is God doesn't desire for any of His children to wallow in the depths of a slimy pit. We are always to be seeking Him and following after Him. After three days, Jonah finally realized this. And his deliverance came as he offered up a prayer of confession and praise.

Today, if you find yourself in a place you know isn't right, read the words of Jonah especially chapter 2. Hear his cry for help. Notice his desire to move out of the pit, and take to heart the deliverance he received. God can do the same for you.

Dear God,
I pray today you would give me a clear vision of the place I am in. Show me if it is a place You have ordained for me or if it is a place I need to flee. Lord change anything in me that needs changing. Search my heart and cleanse me of all unrighteousness. And I ask Lord that You give me a song, a prayer, a cry that will reach Your ears that You may hear and deliver me Lord. Move me forward to the place where You are, to the place You want me to be. Amen.

As I said before we were ready to go somewhere else to find answers. We heard about a muscle movement disorder clinic that was only about three hours away and thankfully they were able to see me right away. The first doctor that came in asked a lot of questions and had me perform several tasks. Then he leaned up against the side of the table and said "I'm almost positive I know what's wrong." He believed that somewhere in my body there was a tumor. It could be so small that it might be very hard to detect. The movements, weakness and all the other unexplained symptoms were my body's way of trying to attack the tumor, but instead it was attacking me. I remember wanting to jump up and down and hug him. My mom was with us, and we just smiled at each other and were so happy to which the doctor replied "I have never seen anybody happy about hearing they may have a tumor". But for us it was an answer. It was something we could fight against. Honestly, it just made me feel a little less crazy. Trust me when your arms start randomly flying through the air and your legs decide to sit down on their own, you feel a little crazy.

A little crazy. Oh that reminds me of a Bible story. Sometimes, when I read the Old Testament my first thought is that's crazy. And I really mean that in a good way. Like the story of Joshua and the Battle of Jericho. Crazy. Here's the short version; the full version you can find in Joshua chapters five and six. The Israelites were to march around the walls of Jericho for seven days, priests play the trumpets and on the last lap on day 7 the army shouts and the walls fall. One word; crazy. Joshua was probably glad it wasn't an election year. He may have been voted out after telling his army the plan. But what's even crazier is that they did it! I mean as far as I know nobody said "so that's your plan, Joshua??" They did it without any hesitation. They carried out the plan exactly as God commanded, and it worked!

Now, don't get me wrong, I'm not surprised that God's plan actually worked. I mean, we are talking about God the Creator, the one who spoke and it was all done. Of course, His plans are going to work. Though I may not like them or like the timing of them, you can bet your bottom dollar they're going to work. So that's not the crazy part. I imagine what seems crazy to people, even to me sometimes, is the singing and the shouting of praise even when faced with an enormous wall that had defeat written all over it. Sometimes, it just seems crazy for us to rejoice in the middle of tough circumstances. Sometimes, it just seems crazy for us to shout praises to God and believe walls will fall. But sometimes, crazy is what we need. The word crazy can mean extremely enthusiastic. As we come against a wall that tries to block the path God has for us, instead of getting frustrated and allowing feelings of fear to take over, try singing. And sing in an extremely enthusiastic way! Go ahead and get your crazy praise on. Because even if that wall doesn't fall, you have moved yourself into a closer position to the Father. Psalm 22:3 says, "He inhabits the praise of His people!" And if I'm going to be facing that kind of wall, then I want God right there with me.

Dear Father,
Help me to sing and shout praises to You no matter what is in front of me. You are always, always worthy of praise. Give me wisdom to know that Your way is the best way for me. Whether You take me through the wall, around the wall or over the wall, teach me to walk in the direction You give. To fully trust You and to live extremely enthusiastically (CRAZY) for You! Amen.

Immediately we began the paperwork for me to be admitted to the hospital. The doctor felt as though all the tests he wanted ordered would be completed faster if I was in the hospital. Some of the tests were a repeat from the earlier hospital stay but he wanted his people to do them and have a look himself. However, there were a couple of new ones. One being a spinal tap. Now, I was all for most of the testing, after all this doctor seemed to have the answer and we were ready to find it. But there was one problem. The next day was my birthday! Who wants to be in the hospital on their birthday?? And the better question is who wants a spinal tap on their birthday?? Ugh.

I had other plans in mind for my birthday. Like eating at my favorite restaurant, not eating hospital food. Spending time with my family, not with nurses and blood pressure cuffs. And I even had a gift in mind, and trust me it was not to have a spinal tap. That was a gift I did not want. Everything in me wanted to reject it.

Romans 6:23 says that eternal life in Jesus is a gift. Jesus Himself is a gift, a gift from God to mankind. A gift to be received, welcomed, held and shared. And yet this most precious gift is rejected. In Acts 4:11, Peter says that Jesus was the stone the builders rejected. Jesus was in the midst of His own people, yet they wanted no part of Him. They didn't want His name to even be spoken.

Then I read Mark 6:1-6. Jesus even admits that He had no honor in His own country. But then for the first time ever I paid attention to verse 5. It says that Jesus "Could not do any mighty works there." Wow. Let that sink in for a minute. Jesus, the son of God, couldn't work. His hands were tied. Why? Verse 6 tells us it was because of their unbelief. You see Jesus didn't come packaged in the gift wrap paper the Jews expected, so they walked away from the gift-giving party. But before you criticize them think about your life, there are times God moves or speaks but not in the way we want or the way we have planned so we reject His way to go our own. In doing so, we reject the gift. And honestly, we too are guilty of unbelief and therefore limiting the power of Jesus in our life. We don't believe He can forgive "that" sin or love "that" person or heal "that" disease. And when we don't believe, it limits the mighty work of Jesus in our life. So, we must ask ourselves, "Do we want the gift or not?" If the answer is yes, then we must live a life of belief, welcoming the gift and freeing Him to work in whatever way He sees best.

Dear Father,

Today, I beg you for a heart, mind and soul that is filled with belief. I pray I will accept your gift of Jesus in my life and never limit the mighty works He has planned. May I never reject You or Your words, but follow You and honor You all of my life. Forgive me for the times I have forgotten this most precious gift and draw me back to You. Work mightily in me and through me, I pray in Jesus name. Amen.

Day 19

After just two short, but eventful days in the hospital, I was sent home. All the test results had not returned, but enough had come back clear and they felt it was okay for me to be discharged. I was told not to return to work, but instead I was to rest and try to regain my strength. They would call me with the final results. And after 3 long weeks of waiting, they finally called.

Once again I was told all the test came back negative which really was a positive thing. But still that didn't explain why my body was going bazerk! Then the doctor began to talk to me about conversion disorder. He told us that stress or a traumatic event can cause the body to act in different ways. For example, some people that are highly stressed have heart attack like symptoms, rush to the emergency room only to find out they're fine, it's just stress. With conversion disorder, the mind is converting the stress or the memory of a traumatic event into a physical problem. And though the physical problem is very real, it does not stem from an identifiable medical issue.

I must admit I didn't believe the diagnosis. I mean, I understand conversion disorder and truly believe it can be a very serious condition. But, I never saw myself as a stressed-out person. It was just hard for me to accept it. But the doctor insisted that this must be the case since nothing was turning up. He encouraged me to go to counseling for the stress and to physical therapy to help with my muscle issues. And, that in just a short time, I will be back to normal. But, what I remember the most about our conversation was right at the end. He said just don't think about it and you will be fine.

Really?? Are you serious?? Don't think about my arms jerking and my legs turning into rubber. Don't think about the tightness in my face or the constant cramping in my left hand? Yep! He was serious. Don't think about it. Ok. Well then, what should I think about?

Philippians 4:8 is the answer. We are to think on "whatever is true, honorable, right, pure, lovely and of good report." And then verse 9 says if we think on those things and live by them then the "God of peace will be with us." How often in life do we get caught up on the negative things? It's easy to do. And it seems those negative thoughts can play over and over again in our minds almost like a broken record. But, God wants to skip that tune and play a new one. He wants us to have a mindset that is filled with hope, filled with the good things He has to offer us. The most important way to keep our mind on those good things is by staying in His word. Only by meditating on His word, on His truth can we have a peace that pushes away the negative and ushers in the positive. Only by thinking on His words can we live an abundant life full of joy. We can control our thoughts if we so choose. And what we are choosing to think on will show in our life. Remember, you get out what you put in. So don't just think on "anything but . . ." Be sure to intentionally think on God and His word.

Dear Father,
So often in my life I am bombarded with negative thoughts, with thoughts that weigh me down and leave me with no hope. I ask You Father to renew my mind. Clear out all the wrong thinking and set my mind on things above.Give me a deep desire for Your word so that it will penetrate my heart and mind. Help me understand that though my problems are very real, by thinking on the peace and goodness of the Lord instead of the issue at hand, only then am I ready to conquer the problems that come my way. Give me the wisdom to know that so many battles are won and lost in the mind. Transform my thinking so that I may live in victory and glorify You. Amen.

After the conversation with the doctor, Chris and I made some decisions. We felt as though I wasn't getting any better at home resting all the time so why not go back to work. Thankfully my position had been held for me. We also decided no counseling for now because I really had no idea what I would even talk about. However we did want to try the physical therapy. So after about two months at home, I returned to work and also went to physical therapy 2 to 3 times per week. The truth is behind all the excitement of returning to work I was really afraid. Afraid of not being able to do the job and really afraid the job itself would add stress to my body. I had a lot of "what-ifs" in my mind.

Have you ever had a case of the "what-ifs?" They can be contagious you know. And boy had I caught them. I was acting like Moses at the burning bush. Moses kept asking the "what if" questions. What if I'm not good enough? What if they ask who You are? What if they don't believe me? What if my speech is a problem? Wait. What? Did Moses really just point out his handicap as if God didn't know he couldn't speak well? Are you serious? Oh yeah. He did.
But just like God had an answer for all the other "what-ifs," God had an answer for this one too. At that moment God remind Moses who had created him and then God even went as far as providing a helper for Moses. It was his own brother, Aaron.

You see God doesn't see you or me as disabled. He knows all the ins and outs of our makeup and He understands that with Him by our side there is nothing that can't be done. He just wants us to see that too. God knew Aaron could speak better, but He still called on Moses to do this job. When I got my pre-k job two years before this illness started, God knew then I would be going through this and yet He still positioned me there. Like Moses' speech impediment, this illness was no surprise.

Once I returned to work I was amazed at the reception given to me. They welcomed me back and encouraged me to keep pressing on. I was truly blessed. I also became fully aware of what a wonderful co-teacher God had placed by my side. She was an Aaron to me, standing by me faithfully, helping me carry out my task. Then I began to hear how I was touching others and changing them because of my determination to work and positive attitude through adversity. Pretty soon I began to see myself as God sees me. Not disabled, but as a limitless possibility in His hands.

Dear Father,
Thank You for allowing me to come to You with all my "what-ifs," but even more, I thank You for having the answers. My questions never stump You. Help me to trust in Your great wisdom and to know that Your plans can not fail. Give me the ability to see myself as You see me, to believe that I am fearfully and wonderfully made, able to carry out everything You have planned for me to do. Amen.

# Day 21

Three and a half months had passed by since the onset of my illness. Now it was time to enjoy myself. Relax a little. Eat a lot. It was November. It was Thanksgiving! I LOVE to go back home and visit with my family. It seems I gain strength each time I visit. My grandparents have four children, 13 grandchildren and 16 great-grandchildren with more on the way. When we all get together there is a lot of noise, laughter, sports talk, dare I say gossip, eating and more eating. For me, it's just a happy time.

Over the last few months so many people had reached out to encourage us, to check on us, to meet our needs. This Thanksgiving, I became overwhelmed with thankfulness as I recalled all the outpour of love. Much of it came from immediate family. But then God extended His hand of love and sent dear friends from our church family to bless us. It seemed everywhere Chris and I went, somebody wanted to make a difference. From family, to church, from work, to my physical therapist, one by one people touched our lives. I remember sitting on my papa's bed that day before everyone arrived and just crying. My mom sat beside me rubbing my back, wiping my tears. I didn't want my illness to be the focus that day. I didn't want anyone worrying over me. I just simply wanted to celebrate all the great blessings from God. I really wanted it to be Thanksgiving time.

Have you ever reached that point? Have you ever just stopped in the middle of the chaos, the storm and found something to thank God for? There is something. I promise you there is always something. I mean I wasn't any better physically and still had no answers. Yet everything in me cried, "I'm thankful, I am so thankful." Sometimes it's so hard to see past the pain, the trouble. But having a thankful heart can get you there. So even if you can't see anything changing for the good around you, then I challenge you to thank Him for things unseen. Thank Him for His love, mercy, grace and forgiveness. Thank Him for salvation. Thank Him for the place He is preparing for you. God is always at work in our life. Though we may not clearly see His hand, it is there. And for that, I am truly thankful.

Dear God,

In the Book of Psalms there is verse after verse reminding us to thank You. So today, I don't want to ask for anything. I just simply want to say, thank You. Thank You for things seen and unseen. Thank You for salvation through Jesus. Thank You for the comforter, the Holy Spirit. Thank You for calming my fears and giving me a hope for tomorrow. Thank You for creating me, loving me and changing me. Thank You for being God. For being Sovereign. Thank You. Thank You. Thank You. Amen.

# Day 22

Are you or or your family into sports? If not you can skip the devotion because it may not make sense to you. No. Wait. You might need to read it. Even I need to read it a few more times after writing it.

It is basketball season!! (Y E L L! Everybody yell, everybody yell!!) We are such huge basketball fans! In fact, that's how Chris and I met. My uncle would take me to play ball on Sunday afternoons with the guys so I could get better. Chris picked me to be on his team and the rest is history! One smooth pass from him and I was sunk! Our wedding date is the official date you can start practicing. After our rehearsal supper, I went to Midnight Madness at the college I was attending to play in the game. Chris and I both played in high school, and I went on to play in college and coach for a couple years. Now he is the one coaching and even doing some individual training on the side. We love it!

Fast forward to where we are now. Chris is the assistant boys coach as a volunteer at the high school our daughter plays for. I'm one of those crazy mom's/coach's wife in the stands. Trust me, I'm easy to spot. But let's not focus on that. Usually, I'm excited about basketball season. This year not so much. I was worried I wouldn't be able to physically make it to the games, to climb the bleachers and stand and cheer for my girl and for my son who plays in middle school. It was going to be a lot of basketball to attend and I just didn't know if I could do it.

Then it happened, a moment I will never forget. Chris stepped down. He stepped down from something he loved, something he was good at doing, something that brought him a little piece of happiness. Chris stepped down. He stepped down from coaching. He decided I needed him more and was willing to make that sacrifice for me. Let me be honest. Unfortunately, I can be one of those wives who often times can be quick to complain about her man. But since that day I really try to be slower to complain and quicker to compliment. I really try to be slower to fuss and quicker to forgive. I can't say I do it all the time, but I try a lot harder than I use to. Why? Because what Chris did that day was a picture of Jesus. He stepped down.

Read the first two chapters of Matthew and of Luke. Let the Christmas story really sink into your heart and into your mind. Jesus stepped down. He had a glorious position in Heaven. He was seated by the head Creator. He was in the huddles daily with the playmaker to orchestrate moves in Heaven and on Earth. He was praised and worshiped for all His victories. And yet He stepped down. Please understand the words I use are not to come across as disrespectful or in anyway written to humanize God. No words I write will ever be of good enough magnitude or greatness to describe our Lord. But rather my word choice was to make me and hopefully you realize that Jesus had a desired position, and He gave it all up for a most undesirable one. Jesus stepped down to be born in a stable and to die on a cross. If you go anywhere and ask anyone, will anybody say yes those are my most desired, most coveted positions? Will anybody say I would give up anything to have a stable and a cross? No. Only Jesus.

When Chris stepped down it proved to me that at this moment your needs are greater than mine. It proved to me that he loved me more than the things of this world. It proved to me he wanted to be by my side. It wasn't his words, it was his action of stepping down that spoke volumes. The Bible is more than words on a page. It is the story of the action that God will take for you. Maybe nobody in this world would step up or step down for you. But now you can know that Jesus will. Jesus did. And if you needed him to do it again, He would. You are worth Him leaving Heaven and all of its Glory. You are worth it to Him. Jesus stepped down to prove that He loves you more than His own life.

Dear Jesus,
Thank You for stepping down to show me just how much You love me, to show me that You desire to be with me. Thank You for stepping down so that I may have salvation. Give me strength to step up and be the person You have created me to be. To step up and receive all that You have for me. To realize that this game of life can only be victorious when I walk along side You and carry out the plays You have specifically designed for me to run. Help me to live life to the fullest, always acknowledging You as my Head Coach, as my Savior, as my Deliverer. And to be willing to step down for others that they too may know the greatness of Your love. Amen.

# Day 23

August to January. Five months had come and gone. Boy time flies when you're having fun. Not that I was really having fun but was definitely staying busy between work, physical therapy, more doctor visits, family, ballgames. Whew! Just writing this makes me tired. The two weeks off for Christmas were much needed. But when January came we were back in full swing.

When school started back, I was reminded of an upcoming training I had to attend. I would need to drive 30 miles there and back for a two-day conference. Unfortunately, I was the only paraprofessional in our school that had to attend. I was nervous about going mainly because nobody there would know about my condition. If I needed help would they look at me as if I was crazy or actually lend a helping hand. I guess there was only one way to find out. But thankfully, as soon as I got there I spotted someone I knew. Our kids have been in elementary school together. Praise God! Somebody I can at least sit with and talk to. Can I just say that God always does more than expected and this day was no exception.

You see, this dear friend, took me in. She gathered supplies for me, helped me carry my bag, walked close by my side in case I fell and even got snacks and lunch for me. Why? Two Reasons. One is because she just has a servant's heart. It's just who she is. She is a giving, loving, caring servant. That, I already knew. But the second reason, I found very interesting.

When she saw me and my inability to walk, to speak correctly, when she saw my abnormal movements her mind went back. Not even a year ago her mother had passed away from a most dreadful disease. And every move I made, every consonant I slurred, every limp in my step reminded her of her mother. Finally, she spoke up. She shared with me the name of the disease and how it had taken her mother's life. Please know that she did this reluctantly. She had no desire to scare me or bring my spirit down. It's just that she had seen it before and desperately wanted to help me even if it meant going through the memories of the pain.

Do you know about Simon? Maybe you do, maybe you don't. Read Mark 15:21. It's just one verse, the only one he is mentioned in. As Simon was passing through the country and coming into town he had no idea what task was ahead of him. When all of the sudden, there he was in the midst of it all. Chances are he had seen this before this dreadful way of death. Chances are he had heard the cries as families were torn apart by other crucifixions. And though he probably didn't want to deal with the pain of the memory of the screams, there he was. There he was carrying someone else's cross. The load was almost too heavy and the pain almost too much to bear yet still somehow he had the strength to do it. He wasn't headed to town to do that kind of business. He was suppose to be doing other things. So why was he here? How did this happen?

Can I just give my opinion? Psalms 37:23 tells us that "the steps of the righteous are ordered by God." I believe, though, Simon was completely unaware, his steps that day were ordered by God. You see God knew His son, Jesus, would need help that day carrying the cross. So He sent a servant, a willing servant, to help carry the load.

I know that my friend was sent that day to me. And though seeing me brought her much pain, she was willing to walk alongside me to help carry my cross. Though it wasn't her plan for the day, she went with God's plan over her own. Just as Simon was there in that moment for Jesus, she was there for me. Why? Because God loves me and He knew I needed her. And with all my heart, I believe He will do the same for you. He loves you so much. He will not leave you alone.

Dear Father,
I believe You love me. I believe You are drawing me nearer to You. You are the most Sovereign being. I cannot begin to understand Your ways. But I trust them Lord. And I want to be part of Your plan. I ask that You order my steps. That I would surrender to Your will. And if the opportunity presents itself to carry a heavy load for someone else, God grant me the strength and the servant's heart to do so. Help me to be there for others as You have been there for me. And Father for those times that my load is too heavy, I ask that You send someone to help me that I may finish strong the course You have set before me. I praise You and thank You, Lord. Amen.

# Day 24

Within a couple of days the friend I had reunited with at the training sessions gave me a call. She was able to give me the number to a specialist concerning the disease her mother had. She kept telling me she didn't think I had the same thing. She hoped and prayed I didn't have it, but was just really concerned at how similar the symptoms were. Chris and I decided it was worth looking into. After all, this was a specialist in this disease, so he would know for certain if this was it or not. We needed to at least rule it out. We needed to go to the specialist.

In Matthew 7:7-8, Jesus is telling us to "Ask, seek and knock." You see Jesus wants us to come to Him for everything. He is our spiritual specialist. The term specialist describes someone who is focused and highly knowledgeable in a specific area. There is no one else more focused on you than Jesus. There is no one more knowledgeable about you and your circumstance than Jesus. His hand has been on you from the beginning of time. You were formed by Him, created by Him, given the breath of life by Him. There is not one area in your life He doesn't know and care about. He is your specialist. And each day, it is to your advantage to meet with Him.

These verses can apply to someone who needs salvation or to someone who has been walking with Jesus for a while. You will never, in this life, get to the point where you no longer need to ask, seek and knock. There will always be more we can learn about our great and mighty God. There will always be situations where we need to ask and seek His great wisdom. There will always be someone that needs a brother or sister in Christ to knock on the heart of God through prayer. Look at the world around you. Look at all that is going on. We need the power of God in our personal lives and in the life of all of the world.

For my own peace of mind I needed to go to the specialist. I needed to ask for a diagnosis, seek treatment, if necessary, and continue to knock on God's door for healing. It was a scary step to take but once we took it, we were glad we did. The same applies in our spiritual life. Yes, God has placed people in our life that we can go to in times of need, people like the doctors I have been seeing. But make no mistake. God is the ultimate specialist. Always seek Him first. Ask for His wisdom on where to go and who to speak with. Knock on the door of Heaven so that all God has in store for you can be opened. There isn't a situation this Specialist can't handle.

Dear Father,
Every time I take a step towards You I am changed for the better. Just being in Your presence impacts every area of my life. I have never regretted spending time with You. So Lord, remind me of that during those times I wander away from You. I ask you now Lord to continue to mold me into Your image. Grant me a strong desire to seek You, not the miracles, not the extra blessings, but You Lord. And as I knock on Your door, I pray Heaven would open up and Your anointing would fall on me. I ask this in Jesus' name. Amen.

You don't have it. Your examination is complete, and you do not have it. Chris and I both let out the long breath we had been holding during the examination. What a relief! We were so thankful this had been ruled out since the prognosis was not good. So now what? While we're here can you help us? What is your opinion? The questions came flooding in. But the doctor was very unsure. Once again, I had stumped a physician. However, he did bring up conversion disorder, making the second doctor to do so. He wanted me to stop working for at least 3 to 6 months, go to a counselor and continue to do physical therapy. He said maybe your mind and body just need a break, maybe you just need to rest.

But, I did not want to stop working. I really enjoyed my job. And I was raised to work. That's what I was taught. So to take time off work because I needed to rest, well that just didn't sound right at all to me. But this had gone on too long for me to not try everything I possibly could. So after talking with my Administration, I took some time off from my job. Then I scheduled appointments for counseling and more appointments for physical therapy. My mindset was, "Let's get this done and move on with my life."

In Isaiah 9:6 there are a list of names for the promised Messiah, Jesus. The very first one is Wonderful Counselor. I had no trouble scheduling my appointment with a counselor. The office was nearby, the cost was partly covered under insurance. The staff and counselor were both friendly and inviting. All in all it was a very good experience. There's no shame in seeking counseling. Proverbs 19:20 says for us to "listen and receive counseling so that we may be wise." Counseling is a good thing. And that's why Jesus is called the Wonderful Counselor. He is available. You never have to worry if His appointment book is too full. He is approachable. He stands ready to listen to all your concerns, fears and frustrations. And He has answers. His words are comforting, healing and full of wisdom.

It's so easy to get overwhelmed by the demands of each day. Often times we get "too busy" to take time out for the One who loves us the most. We allow other things to take top priority in our lives and by doing so we fail to communicate with our Father. Honestly, we need to start saying "no" to things of this world and "yes" to one on one time with the Counselor. The benefits are out of this world! There is such peace and freedom in spending time with Jesus During my time at home I was able to draw nearer to this great and truly Wonderful Counselor. In fact, it was during that time I received the inspiration to write this book. And to this day I am truly thankful that I know where to turn when my soul needs help. Do you?

Dear Father,
I am in awe of the many attributes You have. Thank You for sharing Your great wisdom with me through my journey. There is no situation that You lack knowledge of. Thank You for equipping people with the skills to minister to others in the area of counseling. Remind me of the benefits of sitting at Your feet and taking time to listen to Your words of wisdom. Whether those words come from an earthly counselor, through Your word or even through Your still small voice, I can be changed, encouraged no matter what I am facing. Help me to view counseling not as a sign of my weakness, but as You investing in me to make me the best me I can be! Thank You Jesus, my Wonderful Counselor. Amen.

Finally the end of July came around! Why was I so happy about that?? I have been home. No working. Mostly just going to counseling appointments, physical therapy and okay you got me an occasional lunch date with the hubby. I guess it wasn't all bad. But seriously, if you tell me I have to do something I'd rather just be chilling out in front of the TV. But if you tell me I can't do something, well then I'm trying my best to get up and prove you wrong.

The truth is I was just ready to go to work. Ready to do something. Ready to feel capable of doing something. And the fact that I absolutely loved my job and the incredible staff made the longing even stronger. So I made sure during my six month stay at home to keep in touch with my administration and co-workers. Then came July. I had wondered if I would be able to return to work. The answer? Yes! A big fat, yes!! But let me explain why.

Though I would like to take credit for my return it just wouldn't be right. I mean I have done all that was required of me and I was showing a lot of improvement. Even still, it's not about me. It's about them. You see the administration saved a place for me. Instead of hiring a full-time employee to take my place they were able to hire a long-term substitute during the months I was absent. Yes, I'm speaking in educational terminology, but just shake your head in agreement like you get it. The point is there was a place for me and they had prepared it.

When I learned about this my heart was overflowing with happiness, joy and with great thankfulness! That's the same feeling I get when I read John 14:1-4. Jesus promises us, that He is preparing for us to be with Him. He is clearing out a space for us. I can't wait to see His design plan for my mansion.

But you know Jesus didn't have to do that. He could have just ended everything at the cross. I'm just thinking He could have made it so that we live here forever, and He and the Father reside in heaven. They could even come visit with us from time to time. But for them, that was just not good enough. God our father wants to give us all that He gave His son, Jesus. We have become the sons and daughters of the great King. We are brothers and sisters to Jesus, heirs to the kingdom. Where He is, God wants His children to be. When it is ready, this amazingly beautiful mansion in glory, He will return to bring us home. God always goes further than He has to and I imagine this mansion will be no different.

Dear Jesus,
When You came to earth it was to build a relationship between a fallen world and its holy Creator. Thank You so much for being willing to go to great lengths to bridge that gap. Now, You are busy building again. You're overseeing the construction of our eternal home. Daily, You're adding mansions to our Father's house. Jesus you are such a giver. Thank You so much for what You did way back then and for what You are doing now. Jesus help me to be part of your construction crew. To pour out the foundation of Your word, to build others up. To be a window that others may see the light of Christ. To cover everyone I meet with the love of God. Help me to spread the gospel, this good news that Jesus came, died, rose from the grave and is preparing a place for anyone who will come to Him. Amen.

I quit! I mean I did quit. It is obvious that since you're reading this entry that at some point I quit quitting. Does that make sense? Let me explain. It's been a year since I have written any pages in this book. I know in my heart and my mind and in my very being that God called me to write this book. But I'm just being honest, I got busy. Busy living life. Not in a bragging sense. Believe me there has not been any extravagant traveling going on, no long awaited dream that came true and no not a pay increase that afforded all the luxuries one could ever want. Nope. Just busy. Busy with work. Busy with dishes and laundry. Busy with raising four children, watching my favorite TV shows, cheering on my favorite team, going to church, visiting family, etc. You get the picture. Just busy doing life. I fell back to where I was before I heard the call. Just going through the motions, kinda like Peter.

In John 20, we see that Jesus has been resurrected. (Pause here to give Him praise!) The disciples have gathered together. Mary has told them this amazing life-changing news. When all of the sudden, Jesus comes in the room. (He's really alive! Praise God! ) Verse 21 says that Jesus spoke to them saying "Peace to you. As the Father has sent Me, I also send you."

This is the second time Jesus has specifically called Peter into Ministry. Remember Peter was fishing when Jesus said "Come with Me and I'll make you fishers of men." The call is specific, simple and straight from the mouth of Jesus. But flip to chapter 21 and read verses 1-3. Peter went right back to fishing. Right back to living the life he was living. Is there anything wrong with fishing? Nope. Is there anything wrong with doing the dishes, laundry, ect.? Nope. Is there anything wrong with not following the call of Jesus? Yes.

We all have tasks to do, jobs to fulfill, things we are responsible for. And we are to do those things as unto the Lord. But each of us also has a specific calling and we must know it and live it. You see Peter wasn't called to be a fisherman. He was called to be an evangelist. He could use his knowledge of fishing in his ministry, but fishing wasn't the plan. The plan was for him to preach. I'm so glad Peter didn't catch anything that night. If so, he may have lost sight of the real call on his life. I'm so glad his nets were empty.

Maybe you feel empty now. Could it be that you have forgotten the call on your life and just got caught up in the ordinary things of life. Please hear me. Not everyone is called to leave their job to become a missionary. But, we are *ALL* called to share the good news. The where and the how, well that's where the call of God comes in. Where has He led you? Where has He placed you? How has He opened doors for you to share? What has He prompted you to do? I can't answer those questions. But the Holy Spirit can. He can guide you on the path God has for you.  Speaking of, I need to write another entry.

Dear Holy Spirit,
I pray right now that You would call out to me again. Clearly speak to me whatever it is You have for me to do. And Lord no matter how many times it takes, please keep speaking to me through your Spirit. When I get caught up in life and place Your call on hold, meet me where I am just like you met Peter. Call me to cast out my net on the right side where Your will for me awaits. Bring me back to You. May I remain faithful to carry out Your plans. Amen.

So here I am fall of 2013. 1 year and 3 months after the onset, still no answers. Still struggling day to day. I was back at work as I mentioned earlier, but never really able to work a full week. At this point, I was just trying to figure out how to cope with this illness. I guess trying to figure out how to pace myself at work so I could still be of some value by the time I got home.

It was around this time I got the call. A well known physician, from the town I grew up in, gave me a call. She had been keeping up with my condition through family members. She was very concerned and wanted to reach out to me to help find an answer.

Understand this. It's not that I hung up the phone believing that she was going to have an answer at the moment she saw me or even that she would know the right medicine or a timetable. That's not what made me want to go see her. The fact that she wanted to take on my case when every other physician had pretty much written me off, that's what got me. She had heard my problem and wanted to be a part of the solution.

Do you see how that is a picture of God? When this world has written you off, when situations arise that seem hopeless, God himself is watching, ready to reach out to you. God is pursuing you. He wants to take what may seem as hopeless and breathe new life into the depths of your soul. Romans 5: 7- 9 tell us that God loves us just as we are. It isn't that somehow we healed ourselves of our sinful nature. We didn't wipe away the disease of sin. No, we still carry it. But even so He loves us and He loves us enough to die for us.

It would not have made any sense for this physician to contact me after I am well. No. I needed her in the state I was in. So it is in our relationship with God. He desires us to come as we are so He can do the work. When we try to clean up our act or face situations on our own, we fall short. Only through what Christ did on the cross is there true forgiveness of sin. Only through His shed blood can we be covered in righteousness. Only by His stripes are we healed. He is the true physician seeking and searching to make a difference in your life. He desires to pour out His expertise in your life so that restoration can begin. Will you make an appointment with Him today? Through His word, through His son and through His Holy Spirit God has pursued you.

Dear Father,
Thank You for pursuing me. I pray today that I would see and understand how much You love me. In You, I find acceptance. In You, I feel valued. Lord, there is nothing in this world that is more valuable than a relationship with You. Thank You for calling out to me even in the state that I am in. Lord, I come to You this moment and acknowledge that I am in need of You. I pray I would make more appointments with You so that I may grow in the knowledge of You, grow in love, and grace and mercy. Help me Lord to pursue You as much as You have pursued me. Help me to lay down my life as You did, only living to bring glory and honor to Your name. Amen.

So this physician that pursued me found a clue to what might be going on. She discovered that my muscle enzymes are high. Not sure how that was missed before. I know I have given enough blood that it should have been found. (Shout out to all the nurses who draw blood. No way I could do it. #Ihateneedles)

Okay so great! My muscle enzymes are high! Yay, we know what's wrong and now we can fix it! Well. . . . not exactly. It seems I was way more excited than she was. Basically, we still didn't have any clarity. Having high muscle enzymes can mean a variety of things. So in her words, time will tell.

Ecclesiastes 3:1-8 talk about how there is a time for everything. As I scroll through those scriptures there are times that I don't particularly like. Times I would rather not have to face or go through. Like when it says a time to die. The death of a loved one is so hard to endure. It's almost as if we aren't equipped to handle it. And really we can't except for God giving us the strength to make it through. Then, there is a time to lose. Don't like that one either. We may face the loss of a job we loved, or a home we built, some people lose big Investments they have made, the loss of a friendship, the loss of trust and maybe even hope. We have all gone through times of loss.

As these verses say there are good times and bad. Times we enjoy, times we despise. But the main thing the author of Ecclesiastes is trying to say is that Jesus is Lord of all the times. God is seated on His throne sovereignly, reigning over each and every moment. There is no season or time that He is not over. Verse 11 goes on to say that He, God Himself, makes all these times, these seasons in life, He makes them beautiful in His time.

So when my doctor says time will tell, I must fully trust that God has this season of waiting in His hands. And when time does tell exactly what is going on, He will have hold of that time too. All I need to do now is rest and trust that all my time is in His hands.

I'm not sure what you may be facing, but there is great peace in knowing God is over this time in your life. He is not caught off guard by your circumstance. And He, like my physician, is telling you time will tell. In time, His glory will be revealed to you. In time, His plan will be rolled out as a scroll. In time, His words will tell you of the victory He has ordained for you. Wait patiently for His beautiful outcome to unfold. Our gracious

God and heavenly Father is at work for you. Don't lose heart. Time will tell.

Dear Father,
Sometimes the times in life are hard to bear. Sometimes the times in life are just disappointing. And often times it seems easier for me to focus on those dark times. But Lord help me to see, even in the dark. Open my eyes that I may see every blessing. Open my mind that I may know You are in control. Open my heart that I may feel Your love and presence. God no matter what's going on I give You glory and praise. You are sovereign. You will not forget me. You will see me through this season and bless me as I enter the next season. I pray Your beauty will shine in this time. Amen.

Day 30

It's been almost two years since that physician told me, "Time will tell." During this time, several tests have been administered to see if we can perhaps unravel the mystery. But, here I am, still waiting. The good news is my symptoms have not worsened. So while there can be very bad days there are also very good days.

One of those many tests will haunt me in my dreams for the rest of my life! It was an EMG. If your doctor ever mentions it, run for your life! Okay, maybe it's just me. I do really have a strong hatred and fear for needles. But let me just explain a little. They stick this long needle into your muscle, wiggle it around a bit, then ask you to contract that muscle while they wiggle it some more. Try that 5 times in each arm and see how you like it.

Okay, where was I. Oh, okay. My point. As soon as I could leave the room, tears started pouring down my face. I got to Chris as quickly as I could, and we got out of there even faster. With tears streaming down, I told him no more. No more tests. No more needles. No more blood being drawn. No more. I don't care what's wrong with me. I don't want to know anymore. It's just not worth it.

And then I read 2nd Corinthians 11: 24-28. It quieted me very quickly. In these verses Paul tells of all his trials, his tests, his pain and agony. How in the world could a man survive all these things? The only answer I can give is because he was God's man. Through the power of God that was all over Paul's life, he was able to endure. He was able to say, yeah there's a lot of bad days but there are some good ones and even some great ones yet to come! Interestingly enough back in Romans 8:18 Paul wrote that all those sufferings were nothing when he compared them to the glory that he would see.

If you had a balancing scale and could put good days on one side and bad days on the other which would outweigh the other? Now, let me ask you this. Does it matter? You see if you belong to Christ even the best of days on this earth cannot compare to the glory of Heaven. Test or no test, illness or no illness, shipwrecked or home safe, beaten down or built up, none of it compares to seeing face-to-face our Savior and our Lord.

Dear Jesus,

You have brought me a long way on this journey. You have carried me, walked beside me, defended me, comforted me and strengthened me. Oh God, help me to remember those times, those many faithful times. I pray I will give You praise and thanksgiving for those times. But Lord, set my mind on the things ahead. Keep pushing me forward. Give me a strong desire to run hard this race You have set before me. With all the hills and curves and slippery slopes, Lord they can all be conquered through Your power. I believe Your promise that one day there will be no more sufferings. Place a joy in my heart, a reminder that better days are just ahead. Amen.

Day 31

I sit here almost in tears as I write this last entry. Just a lot of emotions. First of all, I must confess I am often bad about not finishing what I start. So this is a really big deal for me. Secondly, I am sad my Papa and Grandma are not here to celebrate this accomplishment with me. And lastly, I'm just overcome with amazement of what God has brought me and my family through.

I wish I could close this devotional book with an entry entitled "I'm Healed!" Or maybe one that at least gives a name to my illness and the steps I'm taking to cure it. But it just isn't so. Maybe that's for another book.

Since I was little, I have always loved the story of Moses parting the Red Sea. I'm sure some biblical scholar has thought of this before, but as sure as I'm writing this, the Lord just revealed this to me. The Israelites were trapped between the Red Sea and the Egyptians. The parting of the Red Sea has always been the cool part of the story to me. But what God just showed me may change that feeling.

Both the Israelites and the Egyptians were facing the sea. The Israelites must have looked on it as a roadblock, a major setback or maybe even death. The Egyptians must have viewed the sea as an unexpected ally. But oh how their views quickly changed. What the Israelites thought would trap them ended up freeing them. What the Egyptians thought would aid them ended up annihilating them. Turns out neither of their views about the sea mattered. What did matter, was how God viewed the sea.

This illness has been viewed often by me as a sea that may swallow me, washing my very life away. Other times I have viewed this illness as a current drawing me closer to my family and to God. How I view my illness can very much determine what kind of day I have, whether I walk in defeat or thankfulness. Because my view of this illness can change from day today, I must choose to view this from God's eyes. The truth is like the Israelites and the Egyptians, I don't know the outcome. But God does. I don't know how it will be used in my life. But God does. He has my future in full view and that's all that matters.

So whether the waters part before me and set me free from this bondage or whether they end up consuming me, I have peace like a river. The comfort of the Holy Spirit flows through me. The calmness in the voice of Jesus soothes me. And the deep love of God my Father covers me.

Dear Father,

Today I raise my hands over the swirling sea in my life. I raise them in full surrender to Your will. You see the same disturbance that I see, but Your view is more clear, more complete, and more correct than mine. So, Lord, I trust You with my life. Take it. Use it. May everything about me glorify You. Cause me to sink into Your forgiveness, to swim in your grace. Lord, flood my heart and soul and mind with Your word. Teach me to rush to Your side when the waters are high. You Are My strength, my song and my salvation, the rock on which I stand. Amen.

Thank you for allowing me to share my personal journey with you. I pray that in some way you were able to relate my circumstances to yours, but more importantly, to God's word. I pray that in whatever you may be facing, God would reveal Himself to you in a very powerful way. His word is relevant to anything we face today.

If you are not sure of your salvation, I pray today you would surrender your life to Jesus. He was born for you. He was crucified for you. He was raised to new life for you. All of the pain and suffering was for you. All of the power over hell and death was for you. Jesus desires for you to be reunited with your heavenly Father and today can be that day. Romans 10:9-10 says "If you confess with your mouth the Lord Jesus and believe in your heart that God raised Him from the dead, you will be saved. For with the heart one believes unto righteousness, and with the mouth confession is made unto salvation."

Lord, thank You for the opportunity to share the gospel with others who may be facing uncertain circumstances. I pray You bring them peace and fill them with Your presence. May they have a new hope each morning to press in and press on. Jesus, I pray for Your saving power to be over the one who has confessed You as Lord. Reign in their life and make them new. May they know the power of Your salvation. And Holy Spirit, I ask that You use this book to continue to spread the gospel, the good news that Jesus is alive and has great and mighty plans for us. Thank You Father for loving us, for Your salvation and deliverance. I praise You and thank You in Jesus name. Amen.

Made in the USA
Lexington, KY
30 December 2017